CHARLEVOIX PUBLIC LIBRARY
220 CLINTON STREET
CHARLEVOIX, MI 49720

DISCARD

D1418295

DISCARD

J 342.7302 Pric
Price Hossell, Karen
The Articles of
    Confederation

860691000535880

The Articles of Confederation

KAREN PRICE HOSSELL

CHARLEVOIX PUBLIC LIBRARY
220 CLINTON STREET
CHARLEVOIX, MI 49720

Heinemann Library
Chicago, Illinois

© 2004 Heinemann Library
a division of Reed Elsevier Inc.
Chicago, Illinois

Customer Service 888-454-2279

Visit our website at www.heinemannlibrary.com

All rights reserved. No part of this publication may be
reproduced or transmitted in any form or by any means,
electronic or mechanical, including photocopying, recording,
taping, or any information storage and retrieval system,
without permission in writing from the publisher.

Designed by Herman Adler Design
Photo research by Bill Broyles
Printed and bound in the United States by Lake Book
Manufacturing, Inc.

08 07 06 05 04
10 9 8 7 6 5 4 3 2 1

Library of Congress Cataloging-in-Publication Data
Price Hossell, Karen, 1957-
  The Articles of Confederation / Karen Price Hossell.
     p. cm. -- (Historical documents)
Summary: Provides a history of the Articles of Confederation,
explains why they are important, and describes how historical
documents such as this can be restored and preserved.
Includes bibliographical references and index.
  ISBN 1-4034-0800-9 (hardcover) -- ISBN 1-4034-3429-8
(pbk.)
  1. United States. Articles of Confederation--Juvenile
literature. 2. Constitutional history--United States--Juvenile
literature. [1. United States. Articles of Confederation. 2.
Constitutional history.] I. Title. II. Historical documents
(Heinemann Library (Firm))
  KF4508.P75 2003
  342.73'029--dc21

                         2003008191

Acknowledgments
The author and publisher are grateful to the following
for permission to reproduce copyright material:

Cover photographs by (document) Library of Congress;
(portraits, clockwise from top) Stock Montage, North Wind
Picture Archives, Stock Montage, North Wind Picture
Archives; (title bar) Corbis.

Title page (L-R) Library of Congress, Hulton Archive/Getty
Images; p. 4 Richard T. Nowitz/Corbis; p. 5 Justine
Graham/AFP/Getty Images; p. 6 Photo DC; p. 7 Bob
Rowan/Progressive Image/Corbis; pp. 8, 9, 43, 45 National
Archives Records and Administration; pp. 10, 20t, 21, 22t,
23, 25, 26, 28, 36, 39 North Wind Picture Archives; pp. 11,
13, 14, 40 Bettmann/Corbis; pp. 12, 18b, 22b Hulton
Archive/Getty Images; p. 15 National Trust Photographic
Library/Christopher Hurst/Bridgeman Art Library; pp. 16,
37 Art Resource, NY; p. 17 Corbis; pp. 18t, 19b Stock
Montage; p. 19t Independence National Historical Park;
p. 20b Courtesy The Rhode Island Historical Society; pp. 24,
27, 29, 30, 31, 33 Library of Congress; p. 32 Tecmap
Corporation/Eric Curry/Corbis; p. 38 Courtesy of University
of Notre Dame Libraries, Department of Special Collections;
p. 41 Elliott Teel/DC Stock Photo; p. 42 Alex Wong/Getty
Images; p. 44 The Corcoran Gallery of Art/Corbis.

Every effort has been made to contact copyright holders
of any material reproduced in this book. Any omissions will
be rectified in subsequent printings if notice is given to the
publisher.

Some words are shown in bold, **like
this.** You can find out what they mean
by looking in the glossary.

Contents

Recording Important Events

Throughout history, documents have been created by people who wish to make a record of something. Documents are important because they provide a record of significant events. They may reveal how people lived, how major discoveries were made, or what occurred during a war.

Primary sources

When historians are studying what happened in the past, they prefer to use **primary sources.** This term refers to documents that provide a firsthand account of an event. Primary sources can include letters, diaries, newspaper articles, **pamphlets,** and other papers that were written by people who witnessed or were directly involved in an event.

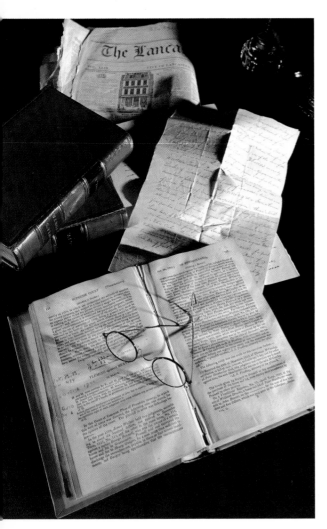

Primary sources can also include official papers that were carefully planned, often with much discussion and argument. The people involved in the planning and writing of these papers were careful to make sure the words in the documents expressed the exact thoughts and ideas they wanted them to. Papers are usually a clear record of just what the authors intended to say.

Primary sources tell us, in the words of the people who lived during that time, what really happened. You can probably come up with something that happened in your own life that

Many examples of primary sources are in this image, including books, letters, and a newspaper.

is important enough to write down. If you only told someone about it instead of writing it down, and that person told someone else, facts could become confused. As the story was passed along again and again, more facts would be confused, changed, or left out. Perhaps something like this has happened to you. When the story comes back to you, you barely recognize it.

This is why primary sources are so important. Over time, facts can be changed or twisted, accidentally or on purpose, so unwritten accounts of what happened in the past can be incorrect. To find out what really happened and why, historians need to rely on primary sources.

Primary sources help people learn more about a particular person or event.

A true sense of history

In this modern day, with so many resources available for sharing information, generating copies, reading text in printed books or on the World Wide Web, maintaining the original documents may seem needless. After all, we do have access to the information they contain. However, the original physical entities [things] convey much more than their intellectual content. The materials used for recording the words, text, and signatures . . . tell us a great deal about the time period in which the documents were created. The original documents also were physically present at the events surrounding their creation, and convey a true sense of history.
— Mary Lynn Ritzenthaler, Chief of the Document Conservation Laboratory at the National Archives and Records Administration, Washington, D.C.

Storing Valuable Documents

Because **primary source** documents provide an important record of historical events, they are considered valuable. For that reason, the paper-and-ink documents are carefully handled and stored so that they will last a long time.

Documents that are considered valuable records of United States history are kept in several different places. The two institutions that hold most of these historical records are the Library of Congress and the National Archives and Records Administration, or NARA.

The Library of Congress

The Library of Congress is in Washington, D.C. It is a **federal** institution and also the largest library in the world. The library holds about 120 million items, including maps, books, and photographs. Its collection is available to members of **Congress** as well as to the rest of the American public.

Inside the Library of Congress are many places where visitors can sit and read.

The NARA building on Constitution Avenue in Washington, D.C., contains many documents that are important parts of U.S. history.

The NARA

The NARA is another government agency. It manages all federal records. Besides paper documents, the NARA also holds films, photographs, posters, sound and video recordings, and other types of government records. The original documents in the NARA collection provide a history of the U.S. government. They also tell the story of American settlement, industry, and farming. In fact, documents and other artifacts detailing almost every aspect of American history can be found in the NARA collection.

Most of the documents at the NARA are stored in specially designed boxes. Since paper is made from plants, it contains acids. Over time, these acids can discolor paper, turning it so dark that the ink on it cannot be read. For this reason, NARA storage boxes are acid-free. The boxes are stored in fireproof, locked **stacks** at the NARA's 41 different facilities. The temperature and **humidity** in NARA storage areas are carefully controlled, because heat and humidity can **deteriorate** documents.

What Are the Articles of Confederation?

The Articles of **Confederation** symbolize an important time in United States history. It is a five-page document that outlines the first government of the United States.

The document is made up of several parts. The first is a paragraph called a **preamble,** which is a kind of introduction. Next are thirteen numbered articles. At the end of the document is a closing paragraph. Below the closing paragraph are the signatures of the 48 **delegates** who approved the Articles of Confederation.

The Articles of Confederation was **drafted** in June and July 1776, at the same time Thomas Jefferson was writing the Declaration of Independence. During those months, members of the Continental **Congress** had decided that the American **colonies** should break all ties with Great Britain and become

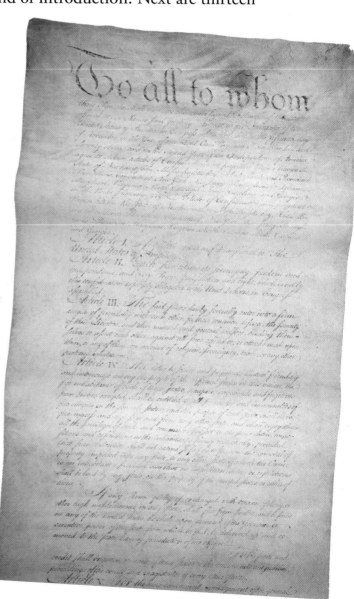

This is the first page of the original Articles of Confederation. Over time, the ink has faded and made the words harder to read.

The Declaration of Independence announced to the world that the American colonies would act together as the United States. It also declared that the U.S. would be free from British rule.

the United States. Congress realized that the new states needed some sort of **pact**, or agreement, to show the world that they were united and able to govern themselves.

Congress named a committee to come up with the agreement. On July 12, 1776, the committee introduced the written articles to Congress. On November 15, 1777, more than a year later, Congress **adopted** the articles. Then a printed version was sent to the thirteen states for approval. It took some of the states a long time to decide to approve the document. So, the Articles of Confederation did not become the official governing document of the United States until 1781—four years later!

Know It

John Dickinson of Delaware led the committee, and he wrote most of the Articles of Confederation.

The Colonial Government

Before the **Revolutionary War,** which took place from 1775 to 1783, the American **colonies** were governed by Great Britain. The thirteen American colonies were all settled primarily by people from Great Britain. Some of the settlers, such as **Quakers** and **Puritans,** came to America because they wanted religious freedom. Other settlers came to seek their fortunes. Spanish settlers had found gold in Mexico and South America, and the British thought they might do the same in the American colonies.

Each colony had its own house of elected representatives who made laws and participated in local government. Britain also sent governors and other leaders to the colonies to oversee them. In addition, the colonies had to follow laws passed by **Parliament,** the British lawmaking body.

Elected representatives of a colony usually got together at town meetings to discuss issues and laws for the colony.

For more than 100 years, this system worked fairly well. As time passed, however, **colonists** began to feel that they could operate independently of Great Britain. Many began to think of themselves as Americans instead of British **citizens**—although, technically, they were still citizens of Great Britain. Colonists felt confident that they could rule themselves.

War and debt

Little changed until the mid-1700s, when a war over rights to land in America broke out between France and Great Britain. The conflict was called the **French and Indian War**, and it lasted seven years. When the war ended in 1763, Britain found that it did not have the money to pay its war **debts**. The war was fought on American soil, with the goal of keeping American colonists safe and protecting British property. So, Britain thought it only fair that the colonists help pay for the war. Parliament decided to tax **goods** it sent to the colonies and use the tax money to pay the debts. In 1764, Parliament passed the Sugar Act, which taxed molasses. In 1765, Parliament imposed the Stamp Act on the colonies. The Stamp Act required Americans to pay to have a special stamp put on many kinds of paper goods when they bought them.

The French and Indian War

The French and Indian War was fought in North America between 1754 and 1763. France and Great Britain fought over land and trade opportunities east of the Mississippi River. Most Native Americans fought on the side of the French, who did not want to move them from their land.

These are a few of the kinds of stamps that colonists had to pay to have put on paper goods after the Stamp Act was passed.

Protesting Taxation

Parliament's decision to require **colonists** to pay taxes made many Americans angry. They believed that people should have a say in the way they were governed. But they had no voice and no vote in Parliament. Parliament was thousands of miles across the Atlantic Ocean, in London, and not one American was allowed to vote at its sessions.

"No taxation without representation"

Many Americans actively protested the taxes. On the streets, in **taverns,** and in town meetings, a popular phrase heard over and over again was "No taxation without representation." In other words, Americans rejected the idea that a law forcing them to pay taxes could be passed by Parliament when they had no vote in Parliament. If colonists went along with this, they believed, they would be no more than slaves to Great Britain. The new taxes would just be the start, and Parliament could make more and more laws for the colonists to obey.

The Stamp Act Congress

Colonists became so concerned over the taxes that they arranged a meeting to discuss what to do. In October 1765, a group of **delegates** from each **colony** met in the Stamp Act **Congress** in New York City. There, they decided to stop buying **goods** from Britain until the Stamp Act was lifted. Most Americans at this time, however, did not want to break away from Great Britain.

American statesman and **patriot** Patrick Henry was strongly opposed to the Stamp Act and worked hard to have the tax **repealed.**

The tea tax

Parliament was surprised at the American protest against the Stamp Act, and in 1766 it repealed, or canceled, the Act. But Parliament immediately passed another act that stated that it did indeed have the right to pass laws for the **colonies** without their representation. Soon after, Parliament passed another act that taxed the colonies. When colonists strongly protested again, Parliament repealed all the new taxes except one—a tax on tea.

On December 16, 1773, to protest the tea tax, a group of men from Boston, Massachusetts, dressed as Mohawk Indians and marched to the dock where ships containing chests of British tea were tied up. The men destroyed every chest of tea on three ships and tossed the tea into Boston Harbor. Soon, people were calling this event the Boston Tea Party.

Boston Tea Party

The Boston Tea Party was the climax of American colonist unrest with British rule. The British were taxing the colonists in order to pay their **debts.** Colonists felt that this was unfair. The Boston Tea Party signaled the beginning of the **Revolutionary War.**

Boston patriots, dressed as Indians, boarded British ships in 1773 and threw chests of tea into Boston Harbor to protest the tea tax. In this image, colonists gathered and cheered on the patriots during the Boston Tea Party.

The Colonies Unite

When **Parliament** found out about the Boston Tea Party, it passed laws called the **Coercive** Acts. The **colonists** called the laws the Intolerable Acts. The acts affected the lives of everyone who lived in Massachusetts—particularly those who lived in Boston. The passage of the Coercive Acts meant that even more British troops moved into the city. Residents of Boston were forced by the Acts to let British soldiers stay in their homes. The soldiers acted as guards to make sure the people of Boston did not have a repeat of the Boston Tea Party.

Boston Harbor closed

Following Parliament's orders, the troops closed Boston Harbor, so only British ships could sail into and out of it. This was a serious move, because most of the **goods** that came into Boston, including food, went through the harbor. To support the people of Massachusetts, other **colonies** began sending cartloads of food and other goods the colonists could not get because the harbor was closed.

The First Continental Congress

The colonial leaders decided that **delegates** from each colony should meet in a Continental **Congress**. In September 1774, the First Continental Congress formed an **association**. The Congress again decided to stop purchasing goods from Britain.

The First Continental Congress met in the Philadelphia State House, also known as Independence Hall, in Philadelphia, Pennsylvania.

The Second Continental Congress

After the First Continental Congress, some delegates tried to get Great Britain's king, George III, to listen to their ideas for a peaceful settlement to the conflict. The king did not respond. So Congress met again in Philadelphia in May 1775 to decide what action to take. This meeting was called the Second Continental Congress.

King George III

Just before Congress met for the second time, British and American soldiers had fought two battles at the towns of Concord and Lexington in Massachusetts. At the Second Continental Congress, delegates decided they had no choice but to declare war on Britain. They selected George Washington to head the Continental Army, and the **Revolutionary War** began.

Congress continued to meet throughout the year and into 1776. By the spring of 1776—a year after the war started—it looked as though there was no way to work out a deal with Britain. It was time for the colonies to take a giant step toward freedom.

Meeting in secret

While colonists knew when the Continental Congress was meeting, what happened in its sessions remained a secret. Delegates even swore an **oath** of secrecy, promising not to discuss what happened during their meetings to anyone outside of the Congress. The main reason for this secrecy was that Congress did not want its enemies—the British—to know how much its members disagreed over certain issues. Congress felt that if the arguments and **debates** that went on during its sessions were known, it would make the **confederation** of states look weak. **Journals** of the meetings were kept, but they contained little information about what happened behind closed doors. Many Americans protested against this secrecy and some Congressional delegates, such as Thomas Jefferson, agreed.

A New Government

On June 7, 1776, Virginia **delegate** Richard Henry Lee stood up in **Congress** to speak. He said that the **colonies** should declare themselves independent from Great Britain. At the same time, he proposed that "[a] plan of **confederation** be prepared and transmitted [sent] to the respective colonies for their consideration and approbation [approval]."

The drafting committee

A committee consisting of one delegate from each colony was named on June 12, 1776, to come up with a plan. Its members were Samuel Adams, Josiah Bartlett, John Dickinson, Button Gwinnett, Joseph Hewes, Stephen Hopkins, Robert R. Livingston, Thomas McKean, Thomas Nelson, Edward Rutledge, Roger Sherman, and Thomas Stone. On June 28, Francis Hopkinson joined the committee.

Benjamin Franklin of Pennsylvania had already developed a plan of confederation in 1775. Congress rejected his plan in that year, but John Dickinson took a copy of it with him to the meetings of the Confederation Committee. He used many of Franklin's ideas in the Articles of Confederation.

Friendly but separate

As committee members set to work, they had to keep one important issue in mind—the colonies felt they had been treated harshly by Great Britain.

Benjamin Franklin

Benjamin Franklin drew this cartoon that shows the American colonies as separate parts of a snake. Just as a snake would die if cut apart, Franklin was showing that the colonies must join together for America to survive.

As the colonies struggled for independence, each colony had become a unit in itself. The residents of each colony felt loyal to their colony first. The colonies were more separate than united in that way, and as they pulled away from Great Britain's power, some colonies had written their own **constitutions.** Each colony wanted to be able to rule itself without **interference** from a strong central government.

Because of these fears, delegates realized that the new government should be one that was a group of friendly but separate states. The men **drafting** the Articles of Confederation knew that was the only kind of confederation all the colonies would agree to.

Know It

Delegates from some colonies wanted to form a strong central government. George Washington, for example, wanted a strong central government right away. The colonies in the South, though, did not. They knew their northern neighbors looked down on their use of slavery. They thought there was a possibility that a **federal** government—one that had power to pass laws that would apply to every colony—would try to outlaw slavery.

The Committee

One **delegate** from each **colony** was selected to be on the committee that **drafted** the Articles of **Confederation**.

Samuel Adams, Massachusetts

Samuel Adams was born in Boston, Massachusetts, in 1722. He was the second cousin of John Adams, the second president of the United States. He ran a **brewery** and was a tax collector, among other things. Adams was also very involved in politics and was a strong supporter of American independence. Some people considered him a troublemaker because he expressed such powerful opinions about American freedom. Adams was the governor of Massachusetts from 1794 to 1797. He died in 1803.

Josiah Bartlett, New Hampshire

Bartlett was born in Massachusetts in 1729 and was a medical doctor. Besides being on the committee to form the Articles of Confederation, Bartlett attended the **Constitutional** Convention in 1787. He was governor of New Hampshire from 1790 to 1794. Bartlett died in 1795.

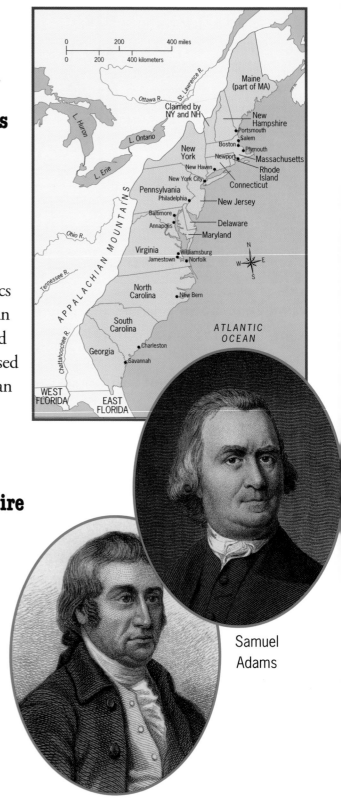

Samuel Adams

Josiah Bartlett

Joseph Hewes, North Carolina

Joseph Hewes was born in New Jersey in 1730. He was a wealthy **merchant** who lived in Philadelphia, and then North Carolina. Hewes was also a commander in the navy. The people of North Carolina elected him to go to the Continental **Congress** in 1774. John Adams said that Hewes "laid the foundation . . . of the American Navy." He died in 1779.

John Dickinson, Pennsylvania

John Dickinson, the chairman of the committee, wrote most of the Articles of Confederation. Dickinson was most likely chosen for the committee because he knew so much about different kinds of government. He was born in Maryland in 1732, but his parents moved to Delaware soon after. Dickinson studied law in Philadelphia, Pennsylvania, and in London, England. Then he became a lawyer in Philadelphia. Dickinson was a member of the Pennsylvania **legislature** and was known as a great speaker.

In 1765, when the colonies were protesting the Stamp Act, Dickinson wrote and published a **pamphlet** that spoke against Britain's use of power. He wrote other works on the subject as well, and became known for his strong views.

While he and the committee were working on the Articles of Confederation, Thomas Jefferson and another committee were writing the Declaration of Independence. After Dickinson read the Declaration, he decided he did not agree with it. He thought Congress should try to find a way to **compromise** with Britain instead of breaking away from it completely. He did not attend the meetings of Congress when independence was voted on, and he did not sign the Declaration. Later, though, he supported the cause of independence. Dickinson died in 1808 in Wilmington, Delaware.

Button Gwinnett, Georgia

Button Gwinnett was born in England in about 1735. Historians are not sure exactly when he moved to Georgia, but believe it was in about 1765. He purchased an island off the coast of Georgia called St. Catherine's. He built a **plantation** there, but lost it when he could not pay his **debts**. He continued to live there, however. Gwinnett did not immediately join the **patriot** cause. In 1775, though, he joined the fight for independence. He helped to write Georgia's state **constitution**. In 1777, he died from wounds he suffered in a **duel**.

Button Gwinnett

Stephen Hopkins, Rhode Island

Hopkins was born in 1707 in Rhode Island. His early career was as a farmer and **surveyor.** In 1731 he entered politics, holding a series of offices, including membership in the state **legislature** and chief justice of the Rhode Island Superior Court. Hopkins was a longtime governor of Rhode Island and a friend of Benjamin Franklin. In fact, he helped Franklin with his plan of **confederation** for the **colonies**. Hopkins spoke out against slavery and was an early supporter of independence for the American colonies. He died in 1785.

Stephen Hopkins

Francis Hopkinson, New Jersey

Francis Hopkinson was a lawyer and a judge from New Jersey. He was also known for his talent for music and writing. Hopkinson was born in 1737. In 1766, he worked as a **customs collector** in England. When he returned to Philadelphia, Pennsylvania, he opened a store, then became customs collector for Delaware. Hopkinson later moved to New Jersey and became a member of its legislature, then a judge. He died in 1790.

Francis Hopkinson

Robert R. Livingston, New York

Livingston was born in New York City in 1746 and later became an attorney. He was also on the committee that wrote the Declaration of Independence. He was the new nation's secretary of foreign affairs from 1781 to 1783. Livingston was very interested in inventing. Unfortunately, none of his inventions worked! So, he is best remembered as a successful statesman and lawyer. Livingston died in 1813.

Robert Livingston

Know It

Livingston helped an inventor named Robert Fulton build the first steamboat. Fulton actually designed and built the boat, while Livingston dealt with all the legal and financial aspects. In 1807, their steamboat made its first trip from New York City to Albany. The invention of the steamboat was a breakthrough in transportation in the nineteenth century.

Thomas McKean, Delaware

Thomas McKean was born in 1734 in Pennsylvania. He was a lawyer and a **delegate** at the Stamp Act **Congress** in 1765. McKean held important positions in both Pennsylvania and Delaware. He represented Delaware in the Continental Congress from its beginning until 1783. In 1777 he was named chief justice of Pennsylvania, a position he held for 22 years. McKean became governor of Pennsylvania in 1799 and held the office until 1808. He died in 1817.

Thomas McKean

Thomas Nelson, Virginia

Nelson was born in 1738 and went to school at Cambridge University in England. He soon became involved in Virginia politics. In July 1775, a convention of Virginia delegates appointed Nelson to represent Virginia in the First Continental Congress. He served as the commander of Virginia's forces in the **Revolutionary War** and is known for his important contributions to the war. Even George Washington praised Nelson after a hard-fought battle. Later, he was governor of Virginia. Nelson died in 1789.

Thomas Nelson

Know It

In May 1777, Nelson became ill with a "disease of the head." No one knows what it was exactly, but it did impair his memory. He recovered, but suffered from the same illness two more times during his political career. After the third time, Nelson was forced to retire from politics.

Edward Rutledge, South Carolina

Edward Rutledge was born in South Carolina in 1749 and studied law in England. He wanted the states to come up with a plan of **confederation** before they announced their independence. Because of that, he did not immediately support breaking away from Great Britain. In 1775, Rutledge, along with Benjamin Franklin and John Adams, went to meet with British military leaders in New York to see if the two countries could come up with a peace plan (which they could not). Rutledge fought in the Revolution, then became a member of the South Carolina **legislature**. In 1798, he was elected governor of South Carolina. He died in 1800.

Edward Rutledge

Roger Sherman, Connecticut

Roger Sherman was born in 1721 in Massachusetts. He was a store owner, and then became a lawyer. Sherman served on several Congressional committees and played a major role in **drafting** the U.S. **Constitution**. He was mayor of New Haven, Connecticut, as well as a U.S. representative and **senator**. He died in 1793.

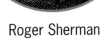

Roger Sherman

Thomas Stone, Maryland

Thomas Stone was born in 1743 in Maryland and was a lawyer. He was not happy about the Revolution. He hoped that the **colonies** would find another way to work out their problems with Britain. Stone was a member of the Continental Congress until 1778, then again in 1784. He then became a Maryland state senator. Stone died in 1787.

Thomas Stone

Forming a Confederation

The committee finished writing the first **draft** of the Articles of **Confederation** on July 12, 1776. After the Articles were presented to the Continental **Congress,** its members agreed that 80 copies should be printed. A Philadelphia printing company owned by John Dunlap and David C. Claypoole did the job. After the copies were printed, they were given to the secretary of Congress, Charles Thomson, who then gave a copy to each **delegate.** He instructed the delegates not to share the document with anyone.

This short news article was printed by Dunlap and Claypoole in 1790.

Philadelphia, Wednesday, June 2.

Congress.

House of Representatives, Monday, May 31.

THE House took up the Resolution proposed by Mr. Fitzsimons, that Congress should meet and hold their next Session at the City of Philadelphia. This motion produced much debate, and finally was agreed to.

Extract of a letter from New-York, June 1.

"I have stolen a moment's leisure, from the hurry of our morning's business, to inform you, that the House of Representatives resolved yesterday, that the next Session of Congress should be held at Philadelphia: For it 38, against it 22."

NEW-YORK, June 1.

Adoption of the Constitution by Rhode-Island.

Yesterday afternoon arrived here, the sloop Rambler, Captain Carey, from Newport, Rhode-Island, who left that place on Sunday morning last:

By the arrival of Captain Carey, we have received the authentic information, that the Convention of Rhode-Island did, on Saturday last, adopt the Constitution of the United States, by a Majority of TWO. The Yeas were thirty-four, the Nays thirty-two.

In the above vessel came passenger Col. Barton, one of the members of the Convention, with dispatches for the President of the United States.

It is expected the Governor of Rhode Island will immediately convene the legislature of that state, in order that they may proceed to the choice of two senators to the Congress of the United States.

Printed by Dunlap and Claypoole.

Congressional debate

Beginning on July 22, Congress **debated** the issues covered in the Articles. One issue was how much power the new government should have. There was also a great deal of debate over how the **colonies** would be represented in Congress. While this debate was continuing, Congress was also discussing when and how to declare independence from Great Britain. As the committee met, Charles Thomson made notes on the original draft written by John Dickinson. Dickinson could not attend the meeting because he had been called to serve temporarily in the Continental Army.

Charles Thomson

On August 20, 1776, a committee made the changes agreed to by Congress. Congress reviewed the changes and then ordered that 80 **revised** copies be printed by Dunlap and Claypoole. The copies were again given to Thomson to distribute, and the instructions for secrecy still applied.

Know It

The notes written by Charles Thomson on the original draft, as well as other notes made by members of Congress during this time, are **primary source** documents. Records such as notes and drafts are a valuable tool for researchers or anyone who wishes to find out what occurred as a document was being developed.

Interrupted by War

While **Congress** realized that the Articles of **Confederation** were important, it set aside discussion of them for quite a while after the August printing. In fact, Congress put off reviewing the Articles until April 8, 1777—seven months later!

The **Revolutionary War** took up most of Congress's time and energy. **Delegates** had to find a way to pay for the war, and find ways to encourage men to join the army. They spent a great deal of time figuring out how to get supplies to the army and other matters related to the war. Also, in late 1776, Congress was forced to move to Baltimore, Maryland, as British forces threatened to take over Philadelphia, Pennsylvania.

Congress returned to Philadelphia in the spring of 1777, and beginning in April set aside two days a week to discuss the Articles. However, delegates were once again distracted as the British threatened to attack Philadelphia. On September 19, 1777, Congress moved to Lancaster,

The Battles of Lexington and Concord, Massachusetts, marked the beginning of the Revolutionary War.

Pennsylvania, then to nearby York. Because matters of war were more immediate, they did not discuss the Articles again until October 8.

Debate resumes

Beginning on October 8, 1777, each issue was reviewed and discussed. The most important issues were how much power Congress should have and how each state should be represented in Congress. Also at issue was how the new government should be set up.

Many members of Congress worried that in the new government, states would have to give up many of their powers. Local government, they felt, knew better than **federal** government how a state should be run. Each state had different needs, and only the state governments knew what those needs were. If there was one government over all the states, then everyone would lose. In effect, the delegates were looking out for their states' interests only, above the interests of the country as a whole.

British troops in Philadelphia

By 1776, the Revolutionary War was in full swing. **Colonists** had decided that it was time that they separated themselves from British rule. During this year, the British got closer and closer to Philadelphia. They eventually captured the city on September 11, 1777.

Thomas Jefferson made these notes during the June 7, 1776, Continental Congress meeting. His notes contain comments on the **debates** on and proceedings of the Declaration of Independence and the Articles of Confederation.

Issues and Concerns

Besides the issue of states' rights, the smaller states were also concerned that the larger states would have more votes in the national **legislature** and therefore have more power. For days, **delegates debated** how states would be represented in the legislature. Those in the larger states, or the more **populous** ones, wanted representation to be based on population. In other words, there would be one delegate per so many people—for example, one per 30,000. The smaller states thought this was unfair. Their states did not have as many people, so they would not get as many votes as the larger states. They wanted to have the same number of votes in the legislature as the larger states. The larger states disagreed. The new nation, most thought, should be run as a **republic,** and in a republic, the majority ruled.

The southern states were also concerned that they would lose their voice in the new **confederation.** They had fewer people because they were made up mostly of farmland. Their delegates worried that because the larger states would have more votes under this system, they would try to outlaw slavery or to tax slave owners for each slave they had.

Slaves greet a **plantation** owner's family in Virginia. The South depended on slaves to do most of their farmwork.

Democracy or republic?

While today the United States is often called a **democracy**, the founding fathers considered their creation to be a republic. In fact, they did not want it to be a democracy at all! In a republic, there are certain laws that cannot change. They are based on moral laws and on what are considered rights given to people by God. Even if the majority of the people wanted to break these laws or put an end to them, they could not. In a democracy, the majority always rules and can make laws based on the will of the people, not based on basic rights or on a particular set of moral laws.

One lawmaking body

Congress also debated whether the legislature of the new government should have one lawmaking body or two. Thomas Jefferson suggested that there be two: a Senate and a House of Representatives. States would have equal representation in the Senate, but the number of delegates per state in the House of Representatives would be based on population. That is the system we use today, but in 1777, Congress voted it down.

Instead, Congress decided to have a unicameral, or one-house, legislation called Congress. Each state could send up to seven delegates to Congress, and was required to send at least two. But no matter what its size, each state would have only one vote in Congress.

This page is from one of the printed copies of the Articles that was distributed to Congress in 1776. The handwritten notes on the page were made by Thomas Jefferson and show changes that were made during meetings of Congress.

Congress Approves the Articles

On November 10, 1777, three people were appointed by **Congress** to carefully review the Articles and to report back whether they thought any more changes should be made. The men on this committee were James Duane, Richard Law, and Richard Henry Lee. On the next day the men presented seven changes. Congress rejected most of them, but a few changes were made.

Another three-man committee was named by Congress on November 13. Duane and Lee were also on this committee. The third member was James Lovell. They were told to make the new changes, and then put the Articles into a final form that was well organized.

Presented to the states

All members of Congress finally came to an agreement about the Articles of **Confederation** on November 15, 1777. Then the last committee was told to have 300 copies printed and to give the copies to Charles Thomson. At this time, Congress was still meeting in York, Pennsylvania, so Frances Bailey of nearby Lancaster did the printing.

Alexander Purdie printed this version of the Articles in Williamsburg, Virginia, in 1777. Purdie also published a newspaper called the *Virginia Gazette*.

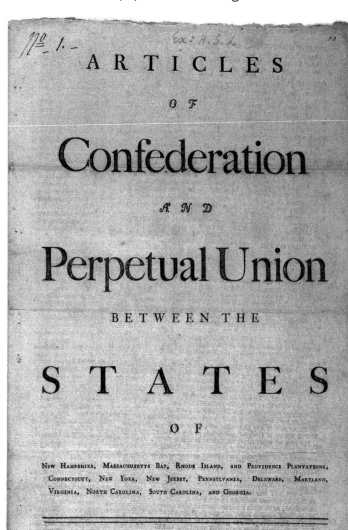

ARTICLES

OF

Confederation

AND

Perpetual Union

BETWEEN THE

STATES

OF

New Hampshire, Massachusetts Bay, Rhode Island, and Providence Plantations, Connecticut, New York, New Jersey, Pennsylvania, Delaware, Maryland, Virginia, North Carolina, South Carolina, and Georgia.

WILLIAMSBURG:
Printed by ALEXANDER PURDIE.

The Purdie printing of the
Articles of Confederation
was four-pages long,
including the title page.

The committee was told to write a letter, called a circular letter because it was to be sent around the country. The letter would go to the states along with printed copies of the Articles. The committee presented this letter to Congress on November 17. In the letter, states were told that by March 10, 1778, they should vote on whether to accept the Articles.

The copies printed by Bailey were done in the form of 26-page **pamphlets.** On November 28, 1777, each **delegate** received eighteen copies to take to his state. The president of Congress kept the extra copies.

Once states received copies of the Articles, they began printing the document in their newspapers so everyone could read it. Historians know that newspapers in Connecticut, Rhode Island, Massachusetts, New Hampshire, Virginia, and North Carolina printed the Articles of Confederation because copies of these newspapers still exist.

Engrossing the Articles of Confederation

On June 26, 1778, **Congress** ordered that the Articles of **Confederation** be **engrossed**. This means that the Articles were written by hand in ink on a special kind of writing material. The writing material, called parchment, was first used more than 1,000 years ago. It is made from animal skin, usually the skin of a sheep, calf, or goat. All fur or hair is stripped or scraped from the skin. Then it is stretched on a frame and scraped some more. As the skin dries, it becomes strong, like a thin piece of leather.

How a document is engrossed

A writer engrossed the Articles using a fancy, flowing style of lettering called calligraphy. He made faint lines down both sides of the paper so that the document would have even margins. To write, the calligrapher used a quill—

An engrosser would have used parchment, a quill, and an inkwell to write out the Articles.

a feather from a goose, duck, swan, or pheasant. The tip of the feather was cut to a point. The ink used to engross the Articles of Confederation was iron gall ink. This ink is made from several different ingredients, including tannin—which comes from plants—and water.

Know It

There is no record of who engrossed the Articles of Confederation.

Some states ratify the Articles

The calligrapher finished the engrossing in one day, but when members of Congress saw the parchment on June 27, they found mistakes. They ordered another engrossed copy. The new copy was presented to them on July 9. On that day, all **delegates** whose states had by that time **ratified,** or agreed to, the Articles were present. They all signed the engrossed copy of the Articles. Eight states had ratified the Articles by July 9, 1778, although in every state **legislature** there were many objections to the Articles and **debates** over whether to agree to them. Many legislatures wanted **amendments** added, but Congress rejected all of them. The states that ratified by July 9 were Connecticut, Massachusetts, New Hampshire, New York, Pennsylvania, Rhode Island, South Carolina, and Virginia. Not all the states agreed to ratify the Articles as quickly. Ratification turned out to be a long, drawn-out process.

This address to the people of New Hampshire from 1783 raises concerns over the eighth article. It would only be a matter of years before the Articles were replaced with the U.S. **Constitution.**

Maryland Objects

While eight states had **ratified** the Articles of **Confederation** by July 9, 1778, five had not. **Congress** had agreed that the Articles could not take effect until all thirteen states ratified them. By 1779, the **legislatures** of twelve states had agreed to ratify the Articles. However, Maryland did not, and that meant the government set up under the Articles could not officially begin.

Maryland's concerns

The reason Maryland would not approve the Articles of Confederation had to do with land. In those days, borders were often unclear, and some states claimed vast areas of mostly undeveloped land. Virginia,

This map shows the original thirteen **colonies,** as well as the land to the west, called the Northwest Territory. Virginia was the first colony to be settled, so it had the earliest claim to western lands.

the first colony to be settled, for example, claimed all the land west of it to the South Sea—now called the Pacific Ocean. At that time, people were not sure exactly how far west that was. There were no accurate maps of the western United States, since much of the land was wilderness occupied only by Native Americans.

The Maryland legislature declared that before it would ratify the Articles, the states that claimed large plots of land had to give most of it to Congress. Maryland feared that the states would find a way to control the government by using the power they got from owning land, and the money they could get from selling it. Maryland's leaders knew that someday settlers would live in the western wilderness, and populations of states such as Virginia would be huge. Smaller states, like Maryland, would be overwhelmed by the larger ones and would have to surrender their power.

For the public good

The larger states realized that the only way to make sure that the states remained united was to turn over their land claims to Congress. On October 10, 1780, Congress decided that the land it received would be used "for the common benefit" of the United States. In 1781, New York was the first state to give up its holdings. Virginia followed, saying that it did so "for the sake of the public good." The amount of land the large states gave up was larger than the territory in the original thirteen colonies!

Know It

The land surrendered during the ratification process of the Articles of Confederation eventually became the states of Ohio, Indiana, Illinois, Michigan, Wisconsin, and Minnesota. **Federal** law directed that slavery be illegal in all of these states.

The Confederation

On March 1, 1781, the Articles of **Confederation** became the official government of the United States. Today, the U.S. government has three branches: the executive branch, which includes the president and his cabinet; the **legislative** branch, which includes the Senate and the House of Representatives, also called **Congress;** and the judicial branch, which is made up of the court system.

Under the Articles of Confederation, however, the legislature of the government was one lawmaking body called Congress. There was no executive branch—so there was no president—and there was no judicial branch. The Articles also stated that, in important matters, at least nine states had to vote.

During the 1780s, mail usually traveled between cities and states on horseback. When a post-rider reached his destination, he would sound his trumpet to let people know that the mail had arrived.

Powers of Congress

The Articles gave Congress some powers. These included the power to:

- determine war and peace
- send and receive **ambassadors**
- agree to **treaties**
- settle boundary **disputes** between states
- **regulate coinage**
- borrow money
- manage affairs with Native Americans
- create and regulate a post office
- regulate the army and navy
- appoint courts so that crimes committed on the high seas could be tried, such as **piracy.**

John Adams, future president of the United States, was an ambassador to France during the confederation government.

Congress was not given all powers, though. For example, it could not keep an eye on foreign trade or other **commercial** matters. It could not impose taxes on the states, and it could not raise an army. If an army was needed, Congress had to ask each state to supply soldiers. It had to pay to make sure the army had supplies and that soldiers were paid.

Finally, the Articles officially called the **colonies** "states," and gave the new nation the name "The United States of America."

Know It

The U.S. government under the Articles of Confederation set up departments to handle specific areas of government. In 1781, Congress created the Department of Foreign Affairs and a War Department. It also created a Department of Finances and started the first American bank, called the Bank of North America.

The Confederation Weakens

The **Revolutionary War** officially ended in 1783. Representatives from the British and American governments met in Paris, France, to sign a peace **treaty.** However, the next few years were hard ones for the new United States.

Poor economy

One of the biggest problems the young nation had was a poor **economy.** The U.S. government had spent millions of dollars on the war. Now it had very little money to pay its **debts,** build roads, or even pay soldiers who had fought in the Revolution. Under the Articles of **Confederation,** the only way the U.S. government could get more money was to ask the states for it. The states could decide whether they would agree to give money to the **federal** government. Sometimes, state governments would raise money, then decide to keep it for themselves.

No standard currency

Another problem was that the U.S. did not have a universal currency, or system of money. The system Americans are now familiar with, based on the dollar, did not begin until 1792. Some states printed their own money. People who traveled could use the money from their state or money from the state in which they were traveling. They could even use British money or Spanish coins.

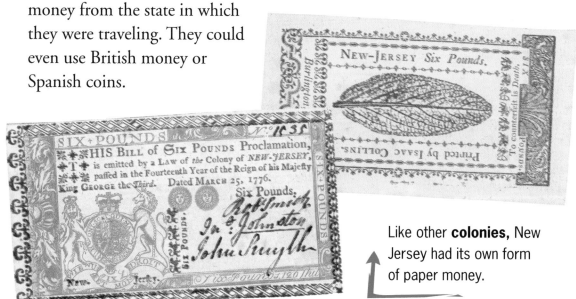

Like other **colonies,** New Jersey had its own form of paper money.

George Washington on the confederation

George Washington was a federalist—he wanted a strong central government for the United States. He wrote of the confederation that "[We] have probably had too good an opinion of human nature in forming our confederation. . . . I do not conceive [think] we can exist long as a nation without having lodged somewhere a power which will pervade [move throughout] the whole Union."

Foreign trade

Foreign trade also became a problem for the U.S. When the colonies were run by the British, they followed British trade laws and customs. But the U.S. was no longer a part of the British Empire, and lost all trade benefits associated with that. According to the Articles, the Confederation government could not create new laws regarding trade with foreign countries. Each state was in charge of making its own foreign trade laws.

Know It

The weaknesses of the Confederation government were not only obvious to Americans. Some European countries were said to be waiting for the Confederation to crumble so they could come in and take over.

Congress tried to make changes to the Articles in order to strengthen them and obtain more power. The changes, called **amendments,** were sent to each state to be voted on. To add amendments, the votes had to be unanimous—that is, every state had to vote "yes." This never happened, so none of Congress's amendments were added.

During colonial times, ports, harbors, and docks were busy with trade ships. The British helped make that possible.

39

The Confederation Ends

Congress realized that it needed to make changes to the way the government was run. So in 1787 it called a meeting to **revise** the Articles of **Confederation.** All of the states knew the government had problems, so each sent **delegates.** At the meeting, called the Constitutional Convention, delegates quickly agreed that instead of revising the Articles of Confederation, they should start over by writing a new **constitution.** The United States Constitution went into effect in 1789, and the confederation of states governed by the Articles of Confederation ended.

This painting depicts the signing of the Constitution in 1787.

The Constitutional Convention

The U.S. Constitution was written in 1787 during the Constitutional Convention. When it was written, the United States had only been around for eleven years. During the Convention, the delegates selected George Washington to be president of the United States.

At the NARA, visitors can see and learn about important **primary sources** relating to U.S. history.

Locations of the original copies

The **engrossed** copy of the Articles of Confederation, written on parchment, is in the National Archives and Records Administration, or NARA, in Washington, D.C. However, it is not on public display. A few of the copies that Congress had printed still exist. The Library of Congress in Washington, D.C., has one of the copies that was printed on July 12, 1776. The NARA has one of the copies that was printed on August 20, 1776. The NARA also has two copies of the August 20 printing that contain notes by delegates. One copy has notes on it that were written by the secretary of Congress, Charles Thomson. The other copy has notes written by John Hancock, who was president of Congress in 1776, and Henry Laurens, who was president of Congress in 1777.

The location of three other printed copies are known as well. One is kept by the Pennsylvania Historical Society, one by the New Hampshire Historical Society, and one by the Library of Congress.

Conserving the Articles of Confederation

The rotunda at the NARA was recently remodeled so that the Charters of Freedom (Declaration of Independence, **Constitution,** and Bill of Rights) would be easier to read and admire. The exhibit reopened in September 2003.

The original, **engrossed** Articles of **Confederation** is kept at the National Archives and Records Administration, or NARA. It is not on permanent display, but sometimes it is included in an exhibit. From December 1997 to December 1998, for example, it was part of an exhibit called "American Originals." This exhibit was shown in the **rotunda** of the NARA in Washington, D.C.

"The Articles of Confederation is stored flat. It is inside a folder and box that are made of high-quality materials that do not contain impurities [harmful or unwanted substances]," explained Mary Lynn Ritzenthaler, who works at the NARA. "The container is closed but not sealed. This protects the document from light but permits air to circulate. This means that the document is not in contact with any material that can damage it." The document is stored in an area with a cool temperature and fairly low **humidity.** These conditions help to preserve the document.

Working at the National Archives

Mary Lynn Ritzenthaler is Chief of the Document Conservation Laboratory at the National Archives and Records Administration (NARA). She manages a staff of document **conservators** whose job it is to repair and restore documents. The conservators also make sure documents are stored so that they will last a long time.

Ms. Ritzenthaler became interested in working with old documents because she always liked old books and loved looking through old papers and documents. Young people who are interested in doing this kind of work, she said, should be able to work well with their hands, because they would be handling fragile papers and books. They should also have an interest in science, since they will need to understand what the materials they are working with are made from and how the materials **degrade** over time.

Ms. Ritzenthaler said that the original Articles of Confederation is in good condition for its age. Before it came to the NARA, it was handled often, so it does show signs of wear. The parchment curls up a little at the edges. At one time, the parchment was probably kept rolled up. In fact, there is a wooden **dowel** attached to the last page of the document. Dowels were usually attached to documents to help a reader roll them up.

Mary Lynn Ritzenthaler

Preserving History

The government under the Articles of **Confederation** only lasted nine years, and many Americans, including George Washington, were unhappy with what it provided. Since it was only in effect for about nine years, the Articles of Confederation may not seem all that important. After all, the United States government is no longer based on the Articles of Confederation. And if we need to read its words, copies of the Articles can be found in books and on the Internet.

But the document itself took months to develop. The men who formed the United States more than 200 years ago argued, discussed, and **debated** for hours and hours about the powers that the Articles of Confederation would give the new government. It represents the ideas of the time and shows how our nation came to be what it is today.

Because we have the original version at the National Archives and Records Administration, we do not have to rely on secondhand information about those times. We have the very ideas of those men, written in their own words.

George Washington, shown here on one of his horses, wanted a stronger United States government than the one provided by the Articles of Confederation.

See the Articles of Confederation

While the Articles of Confederation is rarely on public display, you can see it on the Internet at http://www.ourdocuments.gov/content.php?page=milestone_documents.

The **engrossed** Articles of Confederation holds an important place in U.S. history. It was signed by men who stepped forward to declare that the United States was an independent country with its own government. When we see the document and the signatures, written by the founding fathers with quills on parchment, we can feel closer to them. Their bold measures launched the United States and its people on an exciting journey, one that continues to this day.

Glossary

adopt accept formally and put into effect

ambassador person from one country sent on a government mission to another country

amendment formal change

association group that has formed connections to achieve a common goal

boundary division between two spaces, such as between states

brewery factory that makes beer or other alcoholic beverages

circulate send around

citizen person who lives in a city or town and owes loyalty to a government and is protected by it

coercive bring about by force or threat

coinage system of money based on coins

colonist person who lives in a colony

colony settlement in a new territory that is tied to an established nation

commercial relating to the business of buying and selling

compromise agreement that is the result of two sides giving up something

confederation agreement of support between political bodies

Congress formal meeting of delegates for discussion and usually action on some question; lawmaking body of the U.S. government

conservator person who is responsible for the care, restoration, and repair of documents and other historical artifacts

constitution document that outlines the basic principles of a government

customs collector person who collects fees imposed on goods that are imported or exported

debate argument that follows certain rules

debt amount of money owed

degrade wear down by age, use, or erosion

delegate person sent as a representative to a meeting or conference

democracy system of government in which leaders are elected by the people

deteriorate become damaged in quality, condition, or value

dispute argument

dowel round, wooden stick that fits in a hole on a second piece; used to prevent motion or slipping

draft prepare; unfinished form of a piece of writing

duel battle fought with weapons between two people; duels have formal rules and require witnesses

economy use or management of money

engross prepare the final handwritten or printed text of an official document

federal one central government that oversees smaller units; the smaller units, such as states, also have their own governments

French and Indian War war fought between Great Britain and France in the American colonies from 1756 to 1763; some Native Americans fought with the French, while others fought with the British

good thing that can be bought or sold

humidity amount of moisture, or water, in the air

interfere become involved in the affairs of others

journal written record of daily events

legislative branch of government that makes laws

legislature group of elected individuals who make laws for those who elect them

merchant store owner or trader

oath promise made in front of witnesses

pact agreement between persons, groups, or nations

pamphlet booklet with no cover, usually made of paper folded into smaller parts

Parliament group of elected officials that forms the main ruling body of Great Britain

patriot person who supports his or her country; during the American Revolution, those who fought for freedom from Great Britain

piracy actions of pirates

plantation large farm, usually in the South, often with slaves

populous having a large number of people

preamble introductory statement

primary source original copy of a journal, letter, newspaper, document, or image

Puritan member of a religious group that settled in New England in the sixteenth and seventeenth centuries; Puritans rejected the services of the Church of England as too formal

Quaker member of a religious group called Quakerism that began in the mid-seventeenth century; some Quakers traveled to North America on the *Mayflower* to practice their religion freely

ratify vote to officially approve or accept

regulate govern or control

repeal overrule or dismiss; in Congress, to say "no" to an idea, proposal, or amendment

republic government with an elected head, such as a president, and in which citizens vote for representatives who make laws

revise make changes to

Revolutionary War American fight for independence from British rule between 1775 and 1783

rotunda round building covered by a dome; or large round room

senator elected representative who serves in the senate

stack structure of bookshelves for storing books, often used in libraries

surveyor person who measures land to determine boundaries and geographical features

tavern building in which alcohol is sold; in colonial times, taverns were more like inns, where alcohol and food were sold and rooms were rented out

treaty agreement, often between countries, arrived at after a negotiation process

More Books to Read

Hakim, Joy. *From Colonies to Country.* New York: Oxford University Press Childrens Books, 1999.

Smolinski, Diane. *Important People of the Revolutionary War.* Chicago: Heinemann Library, 2002.

Stein, R. Conrad. *The National Archives.* Danbury, Conn.: Franklin Watts, 2002.

Index